THE STUDENT'S MANGA COOKBOOK

THE STUDENT'S MANGA COOKBOOK

YOUR FAVOURITE RECIPES MADE EASIER THAN EVER...

...WITH STEP-BY-STEP MANGA INSTRUCTIONS!

**YISHAN LI &
CARA FROST-SHARRATT**

ilex

An Hachette UK Company
www.hachette.co.uk

First published in the UK in 2016 by ILEX,
a division of Octopus Publishing Group Ltd
Carmelite House, 50 Victoria Embankment,
London, EC4Y 0DZ
www.octopusbooks.co.uk

Distributed in the US by
Hachette Book Group
1290 Avenue of the Americas, 4th
and 5th Floors, New York, NY 10020

Distributed in Canada by
Canadian Manda Group
664 Annete St., Toronto, Ontario, Canada
M6S 2C8

Publisher: Roly Allen
Commissioning Editor: Zara Larcombe
Managing Specialist Editor: Frank Gallaugher
Senior Project Editor: Natalia Price-Cabrera
Editor: Rachel Silverlight
Art Director: Julie Weir
Designer: Ginny Zeal
Assistant Production Manager: Marina Maher

ISBN 978-1-78157-302-0

A CIP catalogue record for this book
is available from the British Library

Printed in China

CONTENTS

VEGETARIAN

SWEET STUFF

INTRODUCTION

As you get ready to leave home and begin a new adventure as a student, chances are you're not worrying about which kitchen appliances to pack, or where your closest farmers' market will be. With more pressing concerns like parties, dating, social clubs...oh and studying...to worry about, food often gets pushed way down the list of priorities.

But in order to enjoy any of the other activities on offer at college, you need to eat – preferably well and regularly. While you can resort to canteen staples, takeout and endless rounds of toast and butter, you'll pretty soon be bored, bloated and broke. If you want to make mealtimes more exciting, you need to have a few go-to recipes under your belt – easy meals that are cheap, quick and easy to prepare.

If you have a phobia of cookbooks and have difficulty following instructions for opening a packet of pasta, fear not. There's been a revolution on the kitchen bookshelf, as we ditch the traditional recipe formula and prepare meals manga-style.

Meet Hungry Hiro, Sue Shi and their culinary cohorts Cat, Squid, Prawn and Pepper. Together they'll take you step-by-step through each recipe, offering tips, advice and a bit of banter along the way. They've chosen a wide selection of foolproof recipes that should see you through every conceivable college situation – from date nights and mate nights, to post-party kitchen raids and that unexpected visit from your parents.

So, even if you're not on first-name terms with the contents of your fridge, and the only time you use a knife is to pierce the lid of a ready-meal, you'll soon be making masterpieces in your kitchen. Your comic-inspired creations will gain you an instant circle of friends, potential partners and your choice of housemates.

KITCHEN KIT

It goes without saying that you'll need some basic equipment for slicing, dicing, cooking and serving your dishes. But don't worry – nothing in the book requires specialist utensils and you should be able to make every recipe with just the essential kitchen equipment.

You'll obviously need a couple of sharp knives and chopping boards for chopping vegetables and cutting meat. Then a couple of saucepans, a frying pan, sieve or colander, vegetable peeler, spatula, wooden spoons and a decent-sized ovenproof dish should see you through most mealtimes. A hand-held blender would be really useful and these aren't expensive but you can manage without if you don't want to sacrifice beer or bill money to kitchen utensils.

The manga way of cooking proves that anyone can rustle up a decent meal with a bunch of everyday ingredients and equipment.

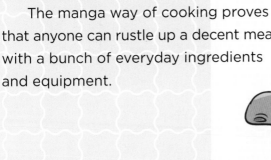

SURF & TURF

TRAY BAKE HERB CHICKEN
A WEEKNIGHT STAPLE THAT USES THE MINIMUM AMOUNT OF EQUIPMENT.

500 G NEW POTATOES
4 BONELESS, SKINLESS CHICKEN BREASTS
6 TBSP CHOPPED HERBS, SUCH AS PARSLEY, CHIVES AND MINT
1 GARLIC CLOVE, FINELY CHOPPED
6 TBSP CRÉME FRAÎCHE
8 BABY LEEKS
2 CHICORY HEADS, HALVED LENGTHWAYS
150 ML CHICKEN STOCK
SALT AND PEPPER
CRUSTY BREAD, TO SERVE

SERVES 4 WARRIORS
PREP TIME: 10 MINUTES
COOKING TIME: 45 MINUTES

COOK THE POTATOES IN A LARGE SAUCEPAN OF LIGHTLY SALTED BOILING WATER FOR 12-15 MINUTES UNTIL TENDER.

DRAIN THE POTATOES THEN CUT INTO BITE-SIZED PIECES.

YOU MIGHT WANT TO LET THE POTATOES *COOL* FOR A MINUTE BEFORE CUTTING.

WHOA, YOU MADE ME *JUMP!*

BET YOU CAN'T MAKE *ME* JUMP.

CUT A SLIT LENGTHWAYS INTO THE SIDE OF EACH CHICKEN BREAST TO MAKE A POCKET.

BE CAREFUL NOT TO CUT RIGHT THROUGH THE CHICKEN OR THE FILLING WILL LEAK OUT.

MIX THE HERBS, GARLIC AND CRÈME FRAÎCHE IN A BOWL WITH SOME SALT AND PEPPER, AND PUT A LITTLE MIXTURE INTO EACH CHICKEN POCKET. KEEP SOME OF THE MIXTURE BACK FOR LATER.

DON'T FORGET TO WASH YOUR HANDS AFTER HANDLING RAW MEAT.

TO PREPARE GARLIC, PUT IT ON A CHOPPING BOARD AND PRESS DOWN WITH THE SIDE OF A KNIFE. THE SKIN SHOULD COME AWAY AND THE GARLIC WILL BE FLATTENED AND EASY TO CHOP.

PREHEAT THE OVEN TO 200°C (400°F), GAS MARK 6. PUT THE LEEKS, CHICORY AND POTATOES IN AN OVENPROOF DISH AND SEASON WITH SALT AND PEPPER.

POUR OVER THE STOCK THEN PLACE THE CHICKEN ON TOP. SPOON OVER THE EXTRA CRÉME FRAÎCHE MIXTURE.

BAKE IN THE PREHEATED OVEN FOR 25-30 MINUTES.

YOU CAN CHECK THE CHICKEN IS COOKED THOUGH BY PIERCING IT WITH A *KNIFE* AND SEEING IF THE JUICES RUN CLEAR.

SERVE THE CHICKEN AND VEGETABLES WITH SOME SAUCE SPOONED OVER THE TOP.

I *LOVE* SOAKING UP THE SAUCE WITH CRUSTY BREAD.

HEY, WAIT TIL I'VE DISHED UP.

VARIATION

BAKED CHICKEN WITH FENNEL & POTATOES

CUT THE COOKED POTATOES IN HALF (INSTEAD OF CUBES) AND PLACE IN A LARGE OVENPROOF DISH WITH 1 LARGE FENNEL BULB, CUT INTO QUARTERS. YOU DON'T NEED THE LEEKS OR CHICORY FOR THIS RECIPE. POUR OVER THE STOCK AND BAKE IN A PREHEATED OVEN AT 200°C (400°F), GAS MARK 6, FOR 20 MINUTES. REMOVE FROM THE OVEN AND PUT THE PLAIN CHICKEN BREASTS ON THE VEGETABLES. MIX 1 TBSP CHOPPED PARSLEY WITH 1 TBSP MUSTARD AND THE CRÉME FRAÎCHE (NO GARLIC), SEASON WITH SALT AND PEPPER AND SPOON OVER THE CHICKEN. BAKE FOR ANOTHER 25-30 MINUTES.

GRILLED CHICKEN SALSA
SPICE UP SUPPERTIME WITH THIS SUPER-EASY CHICKEN DISH.

4 BONELESS, SKINLESS CHICKEN BREASTS
3 TBSP OLIVE OIL
SALT AND PEPPER
BOILED RICE OR SWEET POTATO MASH, TO SERVE

FOR THE CUCUMBER & TOMATO SALSA:
1 RED ONION, FINELY CHOPPED
2 TOMATOES, DESEEDED AND DICED
1 CUCUMBER, FINELY DICED
1 RED CHILLI, FINELY CHOPPED
SMALL HANDFUL OF FRESH CORIANDER, CHOPPED
JUICE OF 1 LIME

SERVES 4 WARRIORS
PREP TIME: 10 MINUTES
COOKING TIME: 10-12 MINUTES

USE KITCHEN SCISSORS TO CUT THROUGH THE WIDTH OF EACH CHICKEN BREAST, WITHOUT CUTTING THE WHOLE WAY THROUGH. OPEN EACH BREAST OUT FLAT.

THIS IS CALLED *'BUTTERFLYING'* AND YOU CAN DO IT WITH PRAWNS TOO... *OUCH!*

BRUSH THE CHICKEN WITH THE OIL AND SEASON WITH SALT AND PEPPER.

PREHEAT THE GRILL TO MEDIUM.

PLACE THE CHICKEN IN A SHALLOW OVENPROOF DISH AND PUT IT UNDER THE GRILL.

YOU SHOULD USE OVEN GLOVES, AS THE GRILL WILL BE *HOT*.

I DON'T HAVE ENOUGH OVEN GLOVES FOR YOU, SQUID!

COOK FOR ABOUT 5-6 MINUTES THEN TURN THE CHICKEN OVER AND COOK FOR ANOTHER 5-6 MINUTES.

MMMM, THAT SMELLS *GOOD*.

JUST WAIT UNTIL IT'S COOKED!

FAST CHICKEN CURRY
THIS IS QUICKER THAN WAITING FOR A TAKEAWAY...AND *MUCH* CHEAPER, TOO

3 TBSP OLIVE OIL
1 ONION, FINELY CHOPPED
4 TBSP MEDIUM CURRY PASTE
8 CHICKEN THIGHS, BONED, SKINNED AND CUT INTO THIN STRIPS
400 G CAN CHOPPED TOMATOES
250 G BROCCOLI, BROKEN INTO SMALL FLORETS,
   STALKS PEELED AND SLICED
100 ML COCONUT MILK
SALT AND PEPPER

TO SERVE:
BOILED RICE
POPPADOMS
MANGO CHUTNEY

SERVES 4 WARRIORS
PREP TIME: 5 MINUTES
COOKING TIME: 25 MINUTES

BRING TO THE BOIL, THEN REDUCE THE HEAT, COVER AND COOK OVER A LOW HEAT FOR 15-20 MINUTES.

AND THAT'S IT?

COOKING REALLY ISN'T THAT DIFFICULT.

WHY DON'T YOU BOIL SOME RICE WHILE THE CURRY'S COOKING? BOYS ARE NO GOOD AT MULTI-TASKING.

MAYBE I LIKE MY CURRY SERVED WITH *NAAN BREAD.*

WELL I LIKE BOTH. RICE IS EASY, JUST FOLLOW THE INSTRUCTIONS ON THE PACKET.

REMOVE FROM THE HEAT, SEASON WELL WITH SALT AND PEPPER AND SERVE IMMEDIATELY.

BET YOU'RE GLAD I COOKED RICE - NOW IT'S A PROPER MEAL.

NOT WITHOUT SOME MANGO CHUTNEY AND POPPADUMS, *YUM!*

IF YOU NEED TO COOL OFF AFTER A HOT CURRY, DRINK MILK, RATHER THAN WATER.

VARIATION

SEAFOOD PATTIES WITH CURRY SAUCE

FOLLOW THE INSTRUCTIONS ABOVE TO COOK THE ONIONS AND CURRY PASTE, THEN ADD THE TOMATOES, 200 G BABY SPINACH LEAVES AND THE COCONUT MILK, AND COOK AS ABOVE.

MEANWHILE, FINELY CHOP 375 G WHITE FISH FILLETS AND 175 G COOKED PEELED PRAWNS. MIX TOGETHER BY HAND.

TRANSFER TO A BOWL, ADD 4 FINELY CHOPPED SPRING ONIONS, 2 TBSP CHOPPED CORIANDER LEAVES, 50 G FRESH WHITE BREADCRUMBS, A SQUEEZE OF LEMON JUICE, 1 BEATEN EGG, AND SALT AND PEPPER.

MIX WELL, THEN FORM INTO 16 PATTIES AND ROLL IN WHITE BREADCRUMBS TO COAT. HEAT ABOUT 1 CM VEGETABLE OIL IN A LARGE FRYING PAN, ADD THE PATTIES IN BATCHES, AND COOK FOR 5 MINUTES ON EACH SIDE OR UNTIL GOLDEN BROWN. SERVE WITH THE CURRY SAUCE.

SPICY MEXICAN BURGERS

BRING THE FLAVOURS OF MEXICO TO YOUR
KITCHEN WITH THESE SIMPLE HOMEMADE BURGERS.

3 TBSP VEGETABLE OIL
1 ONION, FINELY CHOPPED
1 RED PEPPER, CORED, DESEEDED
   AND FINELY CHOPPED
40 G MEXICAN SPICE MIX
   (SUCH AS FAJITA SEASONING)
1 TSP DRIED OREGANO
400 G MINCED BEEF

TO SERVE:
TOASTED BURGER BUNS
GRATED CHEDDAR CHEESE (OPTIONAL)
SPICY SALSA (OPTIONAL)
ICEBERG LETTUCE (OPTIONAL)
GHERKINS (OPTIONAL)

SERVES 4 WARRIORS
PREP TIME: 10 MINUTES
COOKING TIME: 20 MINUTES

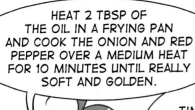
HEAT 2 TBSP OF THE OIL IN A FRYING PAN AND COOK THE ONION AND RED PEPPER OVER A MEDIUM HEAT FOR 10 MINUTES UNTIL REALLY SOFT AND GOLDEN.

THERE'S A TIME AND A PLACE FOR CRISP, CRUNCHY PEPPERS AND A BURGER IS NOT IT...BELIEVE ME, I SHOULD KNOW.

SCRAPE INTO A LARGE BOWL AND SET ASIDE FOR 2-3 MINUTES.

ADD THE REMAINING INGREDIENTS, EXCEPT THE OIL.

MIX ALL THE INGREDIENTS TOGETHER REALLY WELL WITH YOUR HANDS.

THIS IS A *SERIOUSLY* MESSY JOB.

YES BUT IT'S FUN! SHAPE THE MIXTURE INTO 4 EVEN-SIZED BURGERS.

ADD THE REMAINING OIL TO THE PAN AND PLACE IT BACK ON THE HEAT.

MAKE SURE THE OIL HEATS UP BEFORE ADDING THE BURGERS.

COOK THE BURGERS OVER A MEDIUM HEAT FOR 4-5 MINUTES ON EACH SIDE UNTIL COOKED BUT STILL JUICY.

USE A HEATPROOF SPATULA TO FLIP THE BURGERS AND BE CAREFUL OF THE HOT OIL.

IF YOU'VE MADE REALLY THICK PATTIES YOU CAN GIVE THEM AN EXTRA MINUTE TO MAKE SURE THEY'RE COOKED THROUGH.

FORGET THAT, I'M READY FOR MINE NOW.

BE PATIENT - YOU SHOULD ALWAYS MAKE SURE MEAT IS PROPERLY COOKED BEFORE EATING IT.

SERVE THE BURGERS IN TOASTED BURGER BUNS.

I LOVE SOME GRATED CHEESE, SALSA AND LETTUCE WITH MINE.

I'LL JUST TAKE THE BURGER, I DON'T NEED ANY EXTRAS.

HEY, WHO SAID YOU WERE GETTING ANY?!

VARIATION

BEAN TOSTADAS

HEAT A FRYING PAN AND LIGHTLY TOAST A LARGE SOFT TORTILLA WRAP FOR 1 MINUTE ON EACH SIDE. PUSH INTO A DEEP BOWL AND REPEAT WITH 3 MORE TORTILLAS.

MEANWHILE, MIX A 400 G CAN RED KIDNEY BEANS, RINSED AND DRAINED, WITH 1 SMALL FINELY CHOPPED RED ONION, 1 FINELY CHOPPED RED PEPPER, 1 PEELED, STONED AND DICED AVOCADO AND 1 SMALL BUNCH CHOPPED CORIANDER.

DRIZZLE OVER 2 TBSP OIL AND 1 TBSP LIME JUICE AND SEASON WITH SALT. DROP SOME SHREDDED ICEBERG LETTUCE INTO EACH TORTILLA AND DIVIDE THE BEANS BETWEEN THEM. SERVE WITH GRATED CHEDDAR, SALSA AND SOURED CREAM.

BEEF FAJITAS
THE PERFECT DISH TO SHARE
WITH YOUR MATES.

350 G BEEF STIR-FRY STRIPS
40 G PACKET FAJITA SEASONING
4 TBSP VEGETABLE OIL
1 ONION, SLICED
1 RED PEPPER, CORED, DESEEDED AND SLICED
4 LARGE OR 8 SMALL SOFT TORTILLA WRAPS

TO SERVE:
GRATED CHEDDAR CHEESE (OPTIONAL)
JALEPEÑO PEPPERS (OPTIONAL)
SOURED CREAM (OPTIONAL)

SERVES 4 WARRIORS
PREP TIME: 10 MINUTES
COOKING TIME: 10 MINUTES

PUT THE BEEF IN A BOWL AND STIR THROUGH THE SEASONING MIX. SET ASIDE.

MAKE SURE YOU MIX IT IN REALLY WELL SO THE MEAT SOAKS UP THE *FLAVOURS*.

HEAT HALF THE OIL IN A LARGE FRYING PAN AND ADD THE ONION AND PEPPER.

COOK OVER A HIGH HEAT FOR 3-4 MINUTES, STIRRING OCCASIONALLY, UNTIL THE VEGETABLES ARE LIGHTLY CHARRED AND SOFTENED.

CHARRED PEPPERS? I'M NOT SURE I CAN WATCH!

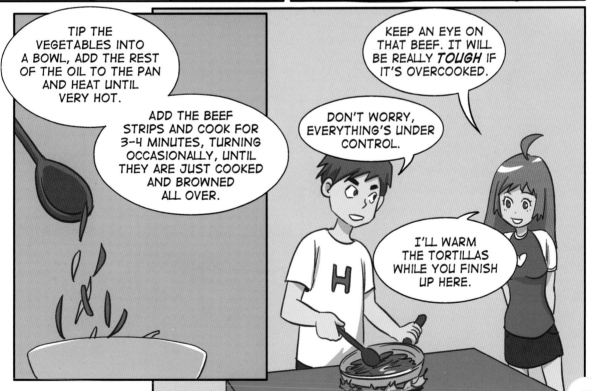

TIP THE VEGETABLES INTO A BOWL, ADD THE REST OF THE OIL TO THE PAN AND HEAT UNTIL VERY HOT.

ADD THE BEEF STRIPS AND COOK FOR 3-4 MINUTES, TURNING OCCASIONALLY, UNTIL THEY ARE JUST COOKED AND BROWNED ALL OVER.

KEEP AN EYE ON THAT BEEF. IT WILL BE REALLY *TOUGH* IF IT'S OVERCOOKED.

DON'T WORRY, EVERYTHING'S UNDER CONTROL.

I'LL WARM THE TORTILLAS WHILE YOU FINISH UP HERE.

MEATBALL TAGINE

THIS DISH IS FROM MOROCCO WHERE A LOT OF
THE COOKING IS DONE IN A POT CALLED A TAGINE.
BUT DON'T WORRY, IT WILL TASTE JUST AS
GOOD COOKED IN A SAUCEPAN!

2 SMALL ONIONS, FINELY CHOPPED
2 TBSP RAISINS
750 G MINCED BEEF
1 TBSP TOMATO PURÉE
3 TSP CURRY POWDER
3 TBSP OLIVE OIL
½ TSP GROUND CINNAMON
625 G CANNED CHOPPED TOMATOES
JUICE OF ½ LEMON
2 CELERY STICKS, THICKLY SLICED
1 LARGE OR 2 SMALL COURGETTES, ROUGHLY CHOPPED
175 G FROZEN PEAS
SALT AND PEPPER
CORIANDER & APRICOT COUSCOUS OR PLAIN
    COUSCOUS, TO SERVE

SERVES 4 WARRIORS
PREP TIME: 15 MINUTES
COOKING TIME: 40 MINUTES

MIX TOGETHER HALF THE ONIONS, THE RAISINS, MINCED BEEF, TOMATO PURÉE AND CURRY POWDER IN A BOWL. SEASON WELL.

I LIKE THE **SWEET** AND **SAVOURY** FLAVOUR COMBINATION.

USING YOUR HANDS, KNEAD TO COMBINE ALL THE INGREDIENTS.

FORM THE MIXTURE INTO 24 MEATBALLS.

YOU COULD DO WITH SOME MORE **HANDS** - HERE, LET ME HELP.

HEAT 1 TBSP OF THE OIL IN A SAUCEPAN. ADD THE MEATBALLS, A FEW AT A TIME, AND COOK UNTIL BROWNED ALL OVER.

THIS WILL TAKE JUST A FEW MINUTES FOR EACH BATCH, AS YOU'RE JUST SEALING THE MEAT, NOT COOKING IT THROUGH.

BE CAREFUL THE HOT OIL DOESN'T **SPIT** WHEN YOU PUT THE MEATBALLS IN THE PAN.

PLACE A PIECE OF KITCHEN PAPER ON THE PLATE FIRST TO SOAK UP ANY EXTRA OIL FROM THE MEATBALLS.

AS EACH BATCH IS COOKED, REMOVE THEM WITH A SLOTTED SPOON AND PUT THEM ON A PLATE.

TIP OUT THE EXCESS FAT THEN PUT ALL THE MEATBALLS BACK IN THE PAN.

YOU SHOULDN'T POUR FAT DOWN THE *SINK!* SET IT ASIDE IN A SEALED CONTAINER AND PUT IT IN THE BIN WHEN COOL.

ADD THE CINNAMON, TOMATOES AND LEMON JUICE, COVER AND SIMMER FOR 25 MINUTES, UNTIL THE MEATBALLS ARE COOKED.

WHILE THEY COOK, HEAT THE REST OF THE OIL IN A LARGE FRYING PAN, ADD THE CELERY AND COURGETTES AND COOK UNTIL SOFT AND STARTING TO BROWN.

ADD THE PEAS AND COOK FOR 5 MINUTES MORE, UNTIL THE PEAS ARE TENDER.

I *LOVE* THAT YOU CAN COOK PEAS FROM FROZEN.

JUST BEFORE SERVING, STIR THE VEGETABLES INTO THE MEATBALL MIXTURE. SEASON WELL.

ACCOMPANIMENT
CORIANDER & APRICOT COUSCOUS

PUT 200 G INSTANT COUSCOUS IN A LARGE, HEATPROOF BOWL WITH 50 G CHOPPED READY-TO-EAT DRIED APRICOTS. POUR OVER BOILING VEGETABLE STOCK TO JUST COVER THE COUSCOUS. COVER AND LEAVE FOR 10-12 MINUTES UNTIL THE STOCK HAS BEEN ABSORBED.

MEANWHILE, CHOP 2 LARGE, RIPE TOMATOES AND FINELY CHOP 2 TBSP CORIANDER LEAVES. FLUFF UP THE COUSCOUS WITH A FORK AND TIP INTO A SERVING DISH. STIR IN THE TOMATOES AND CORIANDER WITH 2 TBSP OLIVE OIL. SEASON, MIX WELL AND SERVE WITH THE TAGINE.

CLASSIC BOLOGNESE
EVERYONE NEEDS A BOLOGNESE RECIPE UP THEIR SLEEVE.

25 G UNSALTED BUTTER
1 TBSP OLIVE OIL
1 SMALL ONION, FINELY CHOPPED
2 CELERY STICKS, FINELY CHOPPED
1 CARROT, FINELY CHOPPED
1 BAY LEAF
200 G LEAN MINCED BEEF
200 G LEAN MINCED PORK
150 ML DRY WHITE WINE
2 X 400 G CANS CHOPPED TOMATOES
600 ML CHICKEN STOCK
400 G DRIED TAGLIATELLE OR FETTUCCINE
SALT AND PEPPER

TO SERVE:
FRESHLY GRATED PARMESAN CHEESE
GARLIC BREAD (OPTIONAL)
GREEN SALAD (OPTIONAL)

SERVES 4 WARRIORS
PREP TIME: 10 MINUTES
COOKING TIME: 1¼ HOURS

SHEPHERD'S PIE
THE PERFECT MEAL FOR A
CHILLY WINTER EVENING.

1 TBSP OLIVE OIL
1 ONION, FINELY CHOPPED
1 CARROT, DICED
1 CELERY STICK, DICED
1 TBSP CHOPPED THYME
500 G MINCED LAMB
400 G CAN CHOPPED TOMATOES
4 TBSP TOMATO PURÉE
750 G FLOURY POTATOES,
   PEELED AND CUBED
50 G BUTTER
3 TBSP MILK
75 G CHEDDAR CHEESE, GRATED
SALT AND PEPPER

SERVES 4-6 WARRIORS
PREP TIME: 20 MINUTES
COOKING TIME: 1½ HOURS

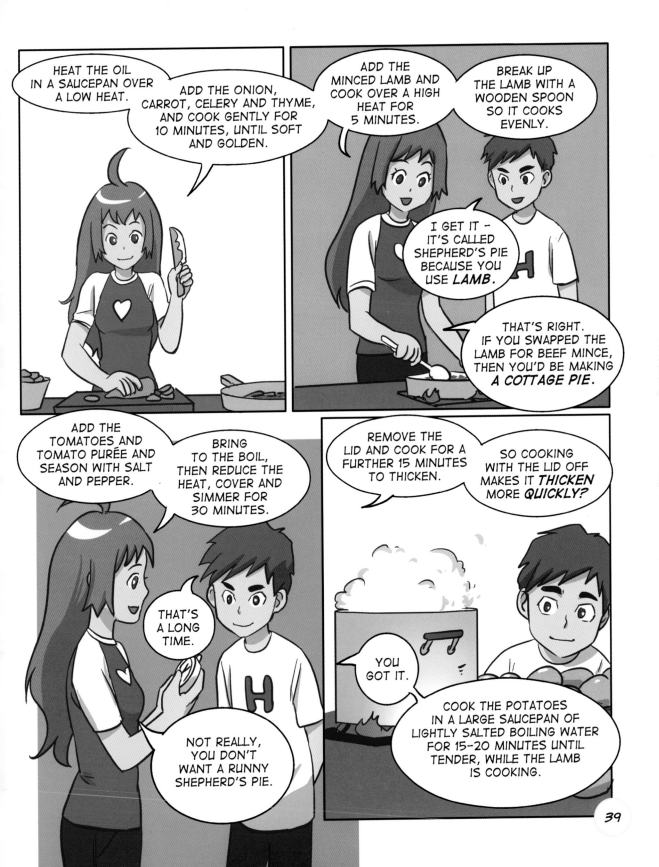

DRAIN THE POTATOES AND RETURN TO THE PAN. MASH IN THE BUTTER, MILK AND HALF THE CHEESE, AND SEASON WITH SALT AND PEPPER.

HEY, MOVE AWAY FROM THE DAIRY!

COME ON, GIVE A CAT A BREAK.

SPOON THE LAMB MIXTURE INTO A 2-LITRE OVENPROOF DISH AND SPOON OVER THE MASH, SPREADING IT EVENLY OVER THE LAMB.

USE A FORK TO FLUFF UP THE MASH, THEN SCATTER OVER THE REST OF THE CHEESE. YOU'LL GET A REALLY NICE, *CRISPY* TOPPING.

GOOD IDEA!

BAKE THE PIE IN A PREHEATED OVEN, 190°C (375°F), GAS MARK 5, FOR 20-25 MINUTES UNTIL BUBBLING AND GOLDEN.

I'M NOT SURE I CAN WAIT THAT LONG, IT SMELLS SO GOOD.

VARIATION

CURRIED LAMB FILO PIES

PREPARE AND COOK THE MINCED MEAT MIXTURE AS ABOVE, ADDING 1 TBSP MEDIUM CURRY PASTE WITH THE TOMATOES AND TOMATO PURÉE.

SPOON THE FILLING INTO SIX 300-ML OVENPROOF DISHES. INSTEAD OF THE POTATO TOPPING, LAYER 4 SHEETS OF FILO PASTRY, ONE ON TOP OF THE OTHER, BRUSHING EACH ONE WITH MELTED BUTTER. CUT THE STACK INTO 6 PIECES AND SCRUNCH EACH ONE OVER A DISH TO COVER THE MEAT.

BAKE IN A PREHEATED OVEN, 190°C (375°F), GAS MARK 5, FOR 20 MINUTES UNTIL THE PASTRY IS LIGHTLY GOLDEN.

SWEET & SOUR PORK
ANOTHER MONEY-SAVING ALTERNATIVE TO A TAKEAWAY MEAL – AND IT WILL TASTE EVEN BETTER, AS YOU MADE IT YOURSELF!

3 TBSP VEGETABLE OIL
350 G CUBED PORK
1 LARGE ONION, CUT INTO
BITE-SIZED PIECES
1 RED OR YELLOW PEPPER, CORED,
DESEEDED AND CUT INTO
BITE-SIZED PIECES
150 G TOMATO KETCHUP
(ABOUT 8 TBSP)
3 TBSP DARK SOFT BROWN SUGAR
225 G CAN PINEAPPLE
CHUNKS IN JUICE
3 TBSP MALT VINEGAR
1 TBSP LIGHT SOY SAUCE
BOILED RICE, TO SERVE

SERVES 4 WARRIORS
PREP TIME: 10 MINUTES
COOKING TIME: 25 MINUTES

HEAT THE OIL IN A LARGE FRYING PAN.

FRY THE PORK OVER A MEDIUM-HIGH HEAT FOR 5-6 MINUTES, UNTIL GOLDEN BROWN ALL OVER.

ADD THE ONION AND PEPPER AND COOK FOR A FURTHER 6-7 MINUTES UNTIL GOLDEN BROWN ALL OVER.

DID YOU SAY PEPPER?

ADD THE KETCHUP, SUGAR, PINEAPPLE AND ITS JUICE, VINEGAR AND SOY SAUCE.

BRING THE INGREDIENTS TO THE BOIL, STIRRING FREQUENTLY.

REDUCE THE HEAT AND SIMMER GENTLY FOR ABOUT 10-12 MINUTES.

IT'S READY WHEN THE SAUCE IS THICK AND THE PORK IS COOKED THROUGH.

YOU CAN ADD *KETCHUP* TO SAUCES, SOUPS, PIE FILLINGS AND CASSEROLES FOR AN *INSTANT TOMATO HIT*.

I'LL BOIL SOME RICE WHILE THAT'S COOKING.

YOU SHOULD HAVE JUST ENOUGH TIME. LONG-GRAIN RICE OR BASMATI RICE WILL GO WELL WITH THIS DISH.

THIS IS THE PERFECT DISH TO PRACTISE YOUR *CHOPSTICK* SKILLS WITH.

LOOKS LIKE YOU MIGHT NEED SOME HELP.

I THINK I'LL SWITCH TO A SPOON.

SERVE THE PORK IN SMALL BOWLS WITH THE RICE IN THE CENTRE OF THE TABLE SO EVERYONE CAN HELP THEMSELVES.

DID YOU GET ANY FORTUNE COOKIES?

NO, BUT I PREDICT EMPTY BOWLS ALL ROUND!

PORK & RED PEPPER CHILLI

THIS IS HOT, SPICY COMFORT FOOD THAT'S PERFECT FOR SHARING.

2 TBSP OLIVE OIL
1 LARGE ONION, CHOPPED
1 RED PEPPER, CORED, DESEEDED AND DICED
2 GARLIC CLOVES, FINELY CHOPPED
450 G MINCED PORK
1 FRESH RED CHILLI, DESEEDED AND FINELY CHOPPED
1 TSP DRIED OREGANO
500 G PASSATA (SIEVED TOMATOES)
400 G CAN RED KIDNEY BEANS, RINSED AND DRAINED
SALT AND PEPPER
ROUGHLY CHOPPED BASIL, TO GARNISH

TO SERVE:
SOURED CREAM
BOILED RICE AND/OR BREAD

SERVES 4 WARRIORS
PREP TIME: 10 MINUTES
COOKING TIME: 30 MINUTES

HEAT THE OIL IN A SAUCEPAN OVER A MEDIUM HEAT.

ADD THE ONION AND RED PEPPER AND COOK FOR 5 MINUTES UNTIL SOFT AND STARTING TO BROWN.

ADD THE GARLIC AND COOK FOR ANOTHER 30 SECONDS OR SO.

MAKE SURE YOU STIR CONSTANTLY WITH A WOODEN SPOON SO THE INGREDIENTS DON'T CATCH ON THE PAN.

ADD THE MINCED PORK AND COOK, STIRRING AND BREAKING UP THE MEAT WITH A WOODEN SPOON.

COOK FOR 5 MINUTES OR UNTIL THE MEAT IS BROWNED.

ADD THE REMAINING INGREDIENTS, SEASON WELL, AND BRING TO THE BOIL.

IF YOU CAN STAND THE HEAT, CHOOSE SMALLER CHILLIES, AS THEY TEND TO BE *HOTTER*.

REDUCE THE HEAT AND SIMMER GENTLY FOR 20 MINUTES.

REMOVE FROM THE HEAT AND SEASON WELL WITH SALT AND PEPPER.

I LIKE FRESHLY GROUND BLACK PEPPER BUT WHITE PEPPER WORKS WELL, TOO.

GARNISH WITH SOME CHOPPED BASIL LEAVES.

IF YOU BUY A *GROWING* POT OF BASIL, YOU CAN USE IT AGAIN FOR OTHER RECIPES.

BUT DON'T FORGET TO WATER IT!

SERVE THE CHILLI WITH SOURED CREAM, BOILED RICE OR CRUSTY BREAD.

KEEP BACK A COUPLE OF SPOONFULS OF CHILLI AND USE IT THE FOLLOWING DAY AS A PIZZA TOPPING, A JACKET POTATO FILLING, OR AS A PASTA SAUCE.

CHILLI PIZZA SOUNDS *AMAZING*.

VARIATION

LAMB & AUBERGINE CHILLI

REPLACE THE RED PEPPER WITH 1 MEDIUM AUBERGINE, CUT INTO SMALL CUBES. FRY AS ABOVE WITH THE ONION AND GARLIC, THEN ADD 450 G MINCED LAMB INSTEAD OF THE PORK.

CONTINUE AS ABOVE. SPRINKLE THE FINISHED DISH WITH 2 TBSP FINELY CHOPPED MINT LEAVES, LEAVE OUT THE SOURED CREAM, AND SERVE WITH BOILED RICE.

SPICY PEA & HAM RISOTTO

THIS IS A HEARTY MEAL THAT'S EASY ON THE WALLET AND TASTES GREAT, TOO.

1 TBSP OLIVE OIL
2 TBSP BUTTER
1 ONION, CHOPPED
1 RED CHILLI, DESEEDED AND FINELY CHOPPED
2 GARLIC CLOVES, FINELY CHOPPED
250 G RISOTTO RICE, SUCH AS
    CARNAROLI OR ARBORIO
900 ML HOT CHICKEN STOCK
200 G FROZEN PEAS
100 G PARMESAN CHEESE, GRATED
300 G COOKED HAM, DICED
BUNCH OF PARSLEY, FINELY CHOPPED
SALT AND PEPPER

SERVES 4 WARRIORS
PREP TIME: 10 MINUTES
COOKING TIME: 30 MINUTES

51

STIR IN THE PARMESAN, HAM AND PARSLEY.

SEASON TO TASTE WITH SALT AND PEPPER.

SAVE A LITTLE PARMESAN TO SPRINKLE OVER JUST BEFORE SERVING.

MMM RISOTTO, ONE OF MY FAVOURITES!

THE *CHEFS* GET THE BIGGEST PORTIONS.

YOU CAN SWAP THE HAM FOR *PRAWNS* IN THIS RECIPE YOU KNOW – JUST ADD A HANDFUL OF COOKED PEELED PRAWNS 5 MINUTES BEFORE YOU FINISH COOKING.

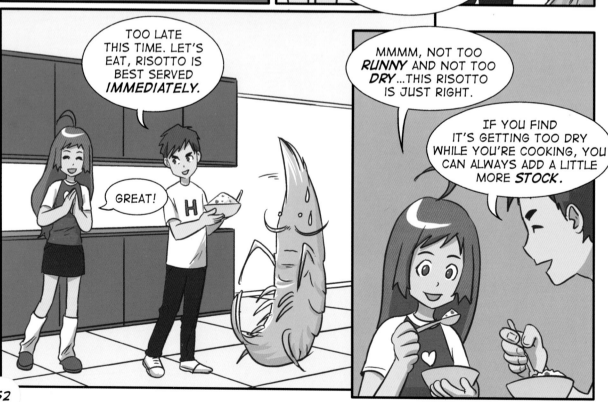

TOO LATE THIS TIME. LET'S EAT, RISOTTO IS BEST SERVED *IMMEDIATELY.*

GREAT!

MMMM, NOT TOO *RUNNY* AND NOT TOO *DRY*...THIS RISOTTO IS JUST RIGHT.

IF YOU FIND IT'S GETTING TOO DRY WHILE YOU'RE COOKING, YOU CAN ALWAYS ADD A LITTLE MORE *STOCK.*

52

POTATO & BACON PATTIES
GIVE YOUR POTATOES A FACELIFT WITH THIS EASY DINNER DISH.

1 KG POTATOES, PEELED AND CUT INTO CHUNKS
1 TBSP VEGETABLE OIL
6 SPRING ONIONS, SLICED
200 G BACK BACON, CHOPPED
2 TBSP CHOPPED PARSLEY
PLAIN FLOUR, FOR COATING
25 G BUTTER
SALT AND PEPPER
STEAMED GREEN VEGETABLES, TO SERVE

FOR THE CREAMY TOMATO SAUCE:
200 ML CRÉME FRAÎCHE
2 TBSP CHOPPED BASIL
2 TBSP CHOPPED TOMATOES

SERVES 4 WARRIORS
PREP TIME: 15 MINUTES, PLUS CHILLING
COOKING TIME: ABOUT 45 MINUTES

COOK THE POTATOES IN A LARGE SAUCEPAN OF LIGHTLY SALTED BOILING WATER FOR 15-20 MINUTES UNTIL TENDER.

THEY NEED TO BE REALLY SOFT OR YOU'LL END UP WITH LUMPY MASH.

YUK, REMINDS ME OF *SCHOOL DINNERS*.

DRAIN THE POTATOES WELL, AND THEN PUT THEM BACK IN THE PAN AND MASH.

YOU CAN ADD A LITTLE MILK TO HELP *LOOSEN* THE POTATOES AND GET A SMOOTHER MASH.

DID SOMEONE MENTION *MILK?*

HEAT THE OIL IN A FRYING PAN, ADD THE SPRING ONIONS AND COOK FOR 2-3 MINUTES, THEN ADD THE BACON AND COOK UNTIL BROWNED.

MMMM THE SMELL OF BACON ALWAYS MAKES ME HUNGRY.

ADD TO THE MASH WITH THE PARSLEY, SEASON TO TASTE AND MIX WELL.

FORM THE POTATO MIXTURE INTO 8 PATTIES, THEN COVER AND CHILL IN THE REFRIGERATOR UNTIL FIRM.

WHY DO YOU NEED TO DO THAT?

SO THEY DON'T *BREAK UP* WHILE YOU'RE HOLDING THEM IN THE NEXT STEP.

PUT THE FLOUR ON A LARGE PLATE AND LIGHTLY COAT THE PATTIES IN FLOUR.

MELT THE BUTTER IN A NONSTICK FRYING PAN.

ADD THE PATTIES IN BATCHES, AND COOK OVER A MEDIUM HEAT FOR 4-5 MINUTES ON EACH SIDE UNTIL BROWNED AND HEATED THROUGH.

WHILE THE PATTIES ARE COOKING, MAKE THE SAUCE.

YOU NEED TO KEEP AN EYE ON THE PATTIES. LET ME HELP.

IT'S EASY – JUST PUT THE CRÈME FRAÎCHE IN A BOWL AND MIX IN THE BASIL AND CHOPPED TOMATOES.

DON'T FORGET TO **SEASON** WITH SALT AND PEPPER.

I WON'T.

SERVE THE PATTIES HOT WITH SOME SAUCE.

IF YOU WANT TO BE **HEALTHY**, STEAM SOME GREEN VEGETABLES TO GO WITH THEM.

SINCE WHEN HAVE YOU BEEN HEALTHY?!

MY BODY'S A **TEMPLE!**

VARIATION

SALMON FISHCAKES WITH SOURED CREAM & MUSHROOM SAUCE

USE A 200 G CAN RED SALMON INSTEAD OF THE BACON. DRAIN AND FLAKE THE SALMON INTO THE MASHED POTATO MIXTURE. FORM INTO CAKES AND COOK AS ABOVE.

MEANWHILE, MELT 25 G BUTTER IN A SAUCEPAN, ADD 100 G SLICED BUTTON MUSHROOMS AND COOK FOR 1 MINUTE.

STIR IN 200 ML SOURED CREAM AND 1/4 TSP PAPRIKA AND SEASON. HEAT THROUGH GENTLY AND SERVE WITH THE FISHCAKES.

MACARONI CHEESE WITH HAM
QUICK-COOK MACARONI MEANS THIS DISH IS READY IN MINUTES.

350 G DRIED QUICK-COOK MACARONI
250 G MASCARPONE CHEESE
100 G CHEDDAR CHEESE, GRATED
100 ML MILK
2 TSP DIJON MUSTARD
400 G CAN PREMIUM CURED HAM,
CUT INTO SMALL CUBES
SALT AND PEPPER
CHOPPED PARSLEY, TO GARNISH
SPINACH WITH OLIVE OIL & LEMON DRESSING, TO SERVE

SERVES 4 WARRIORS
PREP TIME: 5 MINUTES
COOKING TIME: 15 MINUTES

SERVE THE MACARONI WITH THE CHEESE SAUCE SPOONED OVER.

CAN I HAVE MINE WITH THE SAUCE MIXED IN?

SURE, YOU CAN SERVE IT EITHER WAY. JUST FINISH WITH A LITTLE CHOPPED PARSLEY TO GARNISH.

IF YOU HAVE A LITTLE MORE TIME, YOU CAN MIX IN THE SAUCE, POUR IT INTO A DISH, SPRINKLE OVER SOME GRATED CHEESE AND COOK IN THE OVEN FOR ABOUT 15 MINUTES FOR A PASTA BAKE.

SO MANY *OPTIONS!*

MAKE SURE YOU USE A *HEATPROOF DISH!*

AND THIS IS ANOTHER DISH THAT TASTES *GREAT* THE NEXT DAY – *HOT OR COLD*.

YOU SURE LIKE *LEFTOVERS!*

ACCOMPANIMENT

SPINACH WITH OLIVE OIL & LEMON DRESSING

RINSE 625 G SPINACH LEAVES, THEN PUT IN A LARGE SAUCEPAN WITH JUST THE WATER THAT IS CLINGING TO THE LEAVES. SEASON WITH SALT, COVER AND COOK OVER A MEDIUM HEAT FOR 5-7 MINUTES UNTIL WILTED AND TENDER, SHAKING THE PAN FROM TIME TO TIME.

DRAIN IN A COLANDER, THEN RETURN TO THE PAN AND TOSS OVER A HIGH HEAT UNTIL ANY REMAINING WATER HAS EVAPORATED. ADD 2 TBSP BUTTER AND 2 FINELY CHOPPED GARLIC CLOVES, AND MIX WITH THE SPINACH. TRANSFER TO A SERVING DISH, DRIZZLE OVER 4 TBSP OLIVE OIL AND 2 TBSP LEMON JUICE AND SERVE WITH THE MACARONI.

QUICK SAUSAGE & BEAN CASSEROLE

CASSEROLES USUALLY TAKE AGES TO COOK, BUT THIS ONE IS QUICK AND EASY.

2 TBSP OLIVE OIL
16 COCKTAIL SAUSAGES
2 GARLIC CLOVES, FINELY CHOPPED
400 G CAN CHOPPED TOMATOES
400 G CAN BAKED BEANS
200 G CAN MIXED BEANS, DRAINED AND RINSED
½ TSP DRIED THYME
SALT AND PEPPER
3 TBSP CHOPPED PARSLEY, TO GARNISH
MUSTARD MASH, TO SERVE

SERVES 4 WARRIORS
PREP TIME: 5 MINUTES
COOKING TIME: 25 MINUTES

SEASON THE CASSEROLE WITH SALT AND PEPPER.

YOU SHOULDN'T NEED TOO MUCH SALT, AS THE BEANS AND SAUSAGES WILL HAVE SOME ADDED ALREADY.

SERVE THE CASSEROLE HOT, GARNISHED WITH THE CHOPPED PARSLEY.

IF YOU'RE EATING WITH *FRIENDS*, PUT THE DISH ON A HEATPROOF MAT IN THE CENTRE OF THE TABLE AND LET EVERYONE HELP THEMSELVES.

YOU'LL PROBABLY WANT TO SERVE IT WITH AN *ACCOMPANIMENT* AND MUSTARD MASH IS PERFECT.

I'VE GOT A RECIPE FOR THAT – HERE IT IS.

ACCOMPANIMENT

MUSTARD MASH

COOK 1 KG PEELED AND CHOPPED POTATOES IN A LARGE SAUCEPAN OF LIGHTLY SALTED BOILING WATER UNTIL TENDER. DRAIN AND RETURN TO THE PAN. MASH WITH 75 G BUTTER, 1 TBSP WHOLEGRAIN MUSTARD, 3 TSP ENGLISH MUSTARD AND 1 FINELY CHOPPED GARLIC CLOVE. SEASON TO TASTE, THEN BEAT IN 2 TBSP CHOPPED PARSLEY AND A DASH OF OLIVE OIL. SERVE HOT WITH THE SAUSAGE CASSEROLE.

FISH PIE

THIS FISH PIE IS NUTRITIOUS, FILLING AND DELICIOUS.

300 G COOKED PEELED PRAWNS
2 TSP CORNFLOUR
300 G WHITE FISH FILLETS SUCH AS HADDOCK,
   SKINNED AND CUT INTO CHUNKS
2 TSP GREEN PEPPERCORNS IN BRINE, RINSED AND DRAINED
1 SMALL FENNEL BULB, ROUGHLY CHOPPED
1 SMALL LEEK, TRIMMED AND ROUGHLY CHOPPED
15 G DILL
15 G PARSLEY
100 G FRESH OR FROZEN PEAS
350 G READY-MADE CHEESE SAUCE
750 G LARGE POTATOES, PEELED AND THINLY SLICED
75 G CHEDDAR CHEESE, GRATED
SALT AND PEPPER
STEAMED VEGETABLES OR MIXED SALAD, TO SERVE

SERVES 4 WARRIORS
PREP TIME: 15 MINUTES
COOKING TIME: 1 HOUR 10 MINUTES

67

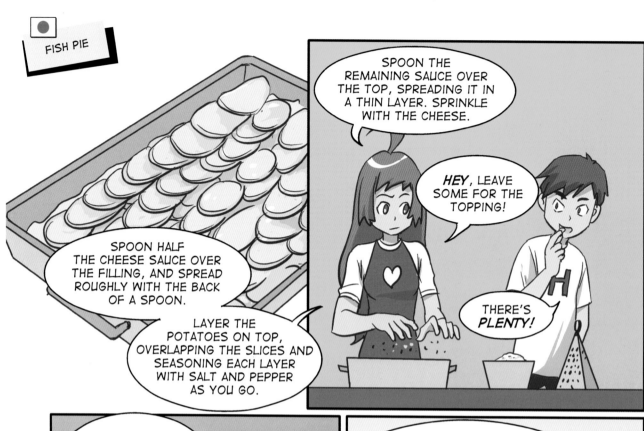

SPOON THE REMAINING SAUCE OVER THE TOP, SPREADING IT IN A THIN LAYER. SPRINKLE WITH THE CHEESE.

HEY, LEAVE SOME FOR THE TOPPING!

THERE'S *PLENTY!*

SPOON HALF THE CHEESE SAUCE OVER THE FILLING, AND SPREAD ROUGHLY WITH THE BACK OF A SPOON.

LAYER THE POTATOES ON TOP, OVERLAPPING THE SLICES AND SEASONING EACH LAYER WITH SALT AND PEPPER AS YOU GO.

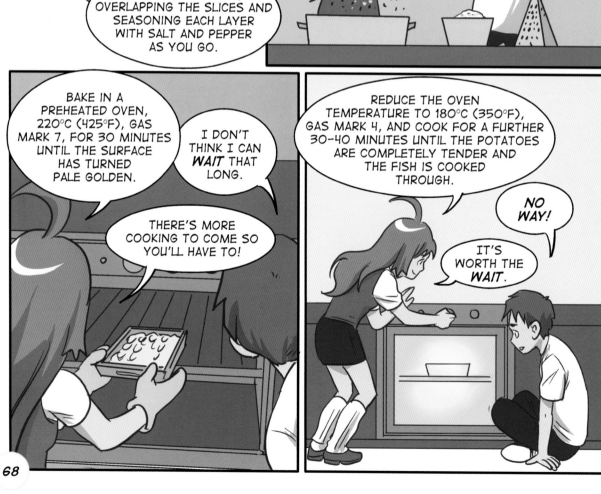

BAKE IN A PREHEATED OVEN, 220°C (425°F), GAS MARK 7, FOR 30 MINUTES UNTIL THE SURFACE HAS TURNED PALE GOLDEN.

I DON'T THINK I CAN *WAIT* THAT LONG.

THERE'S MORE COOKING TO COME SO YOU'LL HAVE TO!

REDUCE THE OVEN TEMPERATURE TO 180°C (350°F), GAS MARK 4, AND COOK FOR A FURTHER 30-40 MINUTES UNTIL THE POTATOES ARE COMPLETELY TENDER AND THE FISH IS COOKED THROUGH.

NO WAY!

IT'S WORTH THE *WAIT*.

SPICY FISH SKEWERS

IF YOU USUALLY CHOOSE LAMB OR CHICKEN FOR SPICY DISHES, WHY NOT TRY FISH FOR A CHANGE?

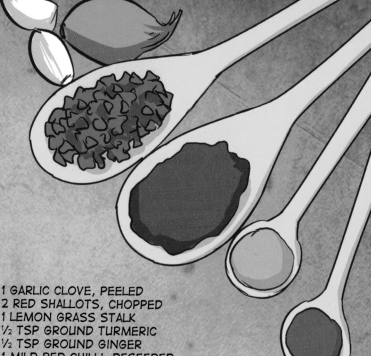

1 GARLIC CLOVE, PEELED
2 RED SHALLOTS, CHOPPED
1 LEMON GRASS STALK
½ TSP GROUND TURMERIC
½ TSP GROUND GINGER
1 MILD RED CHILLI, DESEEDED
    AND ROUGHLY CHOPPED
1 TBSP GROUNDNUT OIL
2 TSP THAI FISH SAUCE
300 G WHITE FISH FILLETS,
    CUT INTO BITE-SIZED PIECES
SALT AND PEPPER
1 TBSP CHOPPED FRESH CORIANDER, TO GARNISH
CHINESE GREENS, TO SERVE

YOU'LL ALSO NEED 4 WOODEN SKEWERS

SERVES 2 WARRIORS
PREP TIME: 10 MINUTES, PLUS MARINATING
COOKING TIME: 5 MINUTES

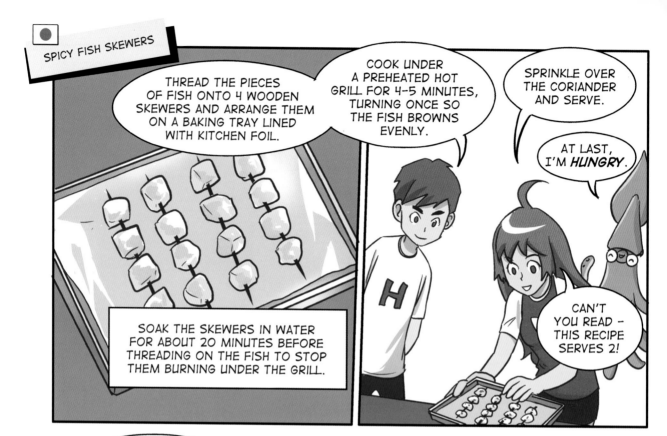

THREAD THE PIECES OF FISH ONTO 4 WOODEN SKEWERS AND ARRANGE THEM ON A BAKING TRAY LINED WITH KITCHEN FOIL.

COOK UNDER A PREHEATED HOT GRILL FOR 4-5 MINUTES, TURNING ONCE SO THE FISH BROWNS EVENLY.

SPRINKLE OVER THE CORIANDER AND SERVE.

AT LAST, I'M *HUNGRY*.

CAN'T YOU READ - THIS RECIPE SERVES 2!

SOAK THE SKEWERS IN WATER FOR ABOUT 20 MINUTES BEFORE THREADING ON THE FISH TO STOP THEM BURNING UNDER THE GRILL.

THESE WOULD BE NICE WITH SOME CHINESE GREENS.

GREAT MINDS THINK ALIKE - CHECK OUT THIS RECIPE.

ACCOMPANIMENT

CHINESE GREENS

PUT 300 G SHREDDED CHINESE GREENS IN A SAUCEPAN OF BOILING WATER AND COOK FOR 1-2 MINUTES. DRAIN WELL AND PLACE ON WARMED SERVING PLATES.

HEAT 1 TSP GROUNDNUT OIL IN A SMALL PAN OVER A LOW HEAT AND COOK ½ TSP FINELY CHOPPED GARLIC FOR 1 MINUTE UNTIL SOFTENED. STIR IN 1 TSP OYSTER SAUCE, 1 TBSP WATER AND ½ TBSP SESAME OIL, THEN BRING TO THE BOIL. POUR OVER THE GREENS.

CREAMY GARLIC MUSSELS
MUSSELS ARE REALLY QUICK AND EASY TO PREPARE BUT LOOK VERY IMPRESSIVE!

1.5 KG FRESH, LIVE MUSSELS
1 TBSP BUTTER
1 ONION, FINELY CHOPPED
6 GARLIC CLOVES, FINELY CHOPPED
100 ML WHITE WINE
150 ML SINGLE CREAM
LARGE HANDFUL OF PARSLEY,
  ROUGHLY CHOPPED
SALT AND PEPPER
CRUSTY BREAD, TO SERVE

SERVES 4 WARRIORS
PREP TIME: 15 MINUTES
COOKING TIME: ABOUT 10 MINUTES

SCRUB THE MUSSELS IN COLD WATER. YOU NEED TO SCRAPE OFF ANY BARNACLES AND PULL AWAY THE HAIRY BEARDS THAT STICK OUT FROM THE SHELLS.

DISCARD ANY MUSSELS WITH **BROKEN SHELLS** OR ANY OPEN MUSSELS THAT DO NOT CLOSE WHEN TAPPED SHARPLY.

MELT THE BUTTER IN A LARGE SAUCEPAN.

ADD THE ONION AND GARLIC AND COOK GENTLY FOR 7 MINUTES UNTIL THE ONION IS TRANSPARENT AND SOFTENED.

ONION NEEDS TO BE REALLY SOFT IF IT'S GOING TO BE PART OF A SAUCE.

INCREASE THE HEAT AND TIP THE MUSSELS AND THE WINE INTO THE PAN.

COVER THE PAN AND COOK FOR 3 MINUTES OR UNTIL THE MUSSEL SHELLS HAVE OPENED.

MAKE SURE YOU THROW OUT ANY THAT STAY CLOSED – THAT MEANS THEY'RE NO GOOD.

I KNOW THAT.

JUST REMINDING YOU.

IT'S EASY BEING AN **ARMCHAIR CHEF.**

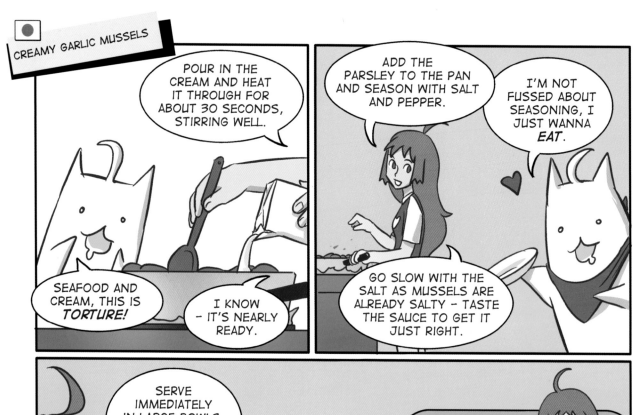

POUR IN THE CREAM AND HEAT IT THROUGH FOR ABOUT 30 SECONDS, STIRRING WELL.

SEAFOOD AND CREAM, THIS IS *TORTURE!*

I KNOW – IT'S NEARLY READY.

ADD THE PARSLEY TO THE PAN AND SEASON WITH SALT AND PEPPER.

I'M NOT FUSSED ABOUT SEASONING, I JUST WANNA *EAT*.

GO SLOW WITH THE SALT AS MUSSELS ARE ALREADY SALTY – TASTE THE SAUCE TO GET IT JUST RIGHT.

SERVE IMMEDIATELY IN LARGE BOWLS, AS THERE WILL BE LOTS OF SAUCE.

AND SERVE WITH PLENTY OF FRESH *CRUSTY BREAD* TO DIP IN THE BOWL.

WOW THIS IS SO GOOD!

VARIATION

MUSSELS IN SPICY TOMATO SAUCE

COOK THE ONION AND GARLIC IN 1 TBSP OLIVE OIL INSTEAD OF THE BUTTER, WITH 1 DESEEDED AND FINELY CHOPPED RED CHILLI. ADD 1 TSP PAPRIKA AND COOK, STIRRING, FOR 1 MINUTE, THEN ADD 400 G CAN CHOPPED TOMATOES.

SEASON TO TASTE WITH SALT AND PEPPER, COVER AND SIMMER GENTLY FOR 15 MINUTES.

MEANWHILE, CLEAN THE MUSSELS, AS ABOVE. STIR THE MUSSELS INTO THE TOMATO SAUCE AND INCREASE THE HEAT. COVER AND COOK FOR 3 MINUTES OR UNTIL ALL THE SHELLS HAVE OPENED. DISCARD ANY THAT REMAIN CLOSED. ADD THE PARSLEY AND SERVE AS ABOVE.

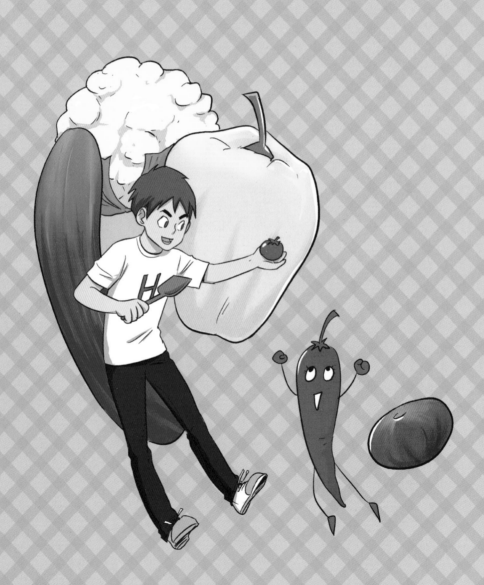

VEGETARIAN

BLACK-EYED BEAN & RED PEPPER STEW
A HEARTY STEW THAT WILL IMPRESS MEAT EATERS TOO.

2 TBSP OLIVE OIL
4 SHALLOTS, FINELY CHOPPED
2 GARLIC CLOVES, FINELY CHOPPED
2 CELERY STICKS, DICED
1 LARGE CARROT, PEELED AND CUT INTO 1 CM PIECES
1 RED PEPPER, CORED, DESEEDED AND CUT
   INTO 1 CM PIECES
1 TSP DRIED MIXED HERBS
2 TSP GROUND CUMIN
1 TSP GROUND CINNAMON
2 X 400 G CANS TOMATOES
2 TBSP SUN-DRIED TOMATO PURÉE
75 ML VEGETABLE STOCK
2 X 400 G CANS BLACK-EYED BEANS
   IN WATER, RINSED AND DRAINED
SALT AND PEPPER
4 TBSP FINELY CHOPPED CORIANDER LEAVES,
   TO GARNISH
BOILED BASMATI RICE, TO SERVE

SERVES 4 WARRIORS
PREP TIME: 20 MINUTES
COOKING TIME: 15-20 MINUTES

HEAT THE OIL IN A LARGE FRYING PAN AND PLACE OVER A HIGH HEAT.

ADD THE SHALLOTS, GARLIC, CELERY, CARROT AND RED PEPPER AND STIR-FRY FOR 2-3 MINUTES OR UNTIL JUST STARTING TO BROWN.

WHAT'S A *SHALLOT?*

IT'S BASICALLY LIKE A SMALL ONION AND IT HAS A REALLY SWEET FLAVOUR.

ADD THE DRIED HERBS, CUMIN, CINNAMON, TOMATOES, TOMATO PURÉE AND STOCK AND BRING TO THE BOIL.

YOU CAN MAKE YOUR OWN VEGETABLE STOCK AND FREEZE IN BATCHES FOR WHEN YOU NEED IT. OR YOU CAN BUY FRESH STOCK FROM THE SUPERMARKET OR USE A STOCK CUBE.

REDUCE THE HEAT TO MEDIUM, COVER AND COOK GENTLY FOR 12-15 MINUTES OR UNTIL THE VEGETABLES ARE TENDER.

BREAK UP THE TOMATOES INTO SMALL PIECES WITH A WOODEN SPOON TOWARDS THE END OF THE COOKING TIME.

WHY DO YOU DO THAT?

IT MAKES THE SAUCE SMOOTH AND HELPS *RELEASE* THE *FLAVOURS*.

YOU CAN BOIL THE RICE WHILE THE STEW IS COOKING.

WE CAN ADD THE BLACK-EYED BEANS NOW.

COOK THESE FOR 2-3 MINUTES UNTIL THEY'RE PIPING HOT.

IT SMELLS *GREAT*.

SEASON WELL WITH SALT AND PEPPER THEN REMOVE THE PAN FROM THE HEAT AND SPRINKLE OVER THE CHOPPED CORIANDER.

CORIANDER ADDS *COLOUR* AS WELL AS FLAVOUR.

I LOVE THIS MEAL.

PUT THE POT OF STEW AND THE RICE ON THE TABLE AND DINNER IS SERVED.

LET'S EAT!

VARIATION

COLOURFUL BLACK-EYED BEAN & VEGETABLE SALAD

FINELY CHOP 2 CARROTS, 2 CELERY STICKS, 1 RED PEPPER, 2 TOMATOES AND 2 SHALLOTS AND PLACE IN A BOWL WITH 4 TBSP OLIVE OIL AND THE JUICE OF 2 LIMES. SEASON AND ADD A 400 G CAN BLACK-EYED BEANS, RINSED AND DRAINED, AND A LARGE HANDFUL OF CHOPPED CORIANDER AND MINT LEAVES. TOSS TO MIX WELL AND SERVE WITH WARM FLATBREADS.

VARIATION

HEARTY BEAN & VEGETABLE BROTH

PLACE 1 FINELY DICED CARROT, 2 FINELY DICED CELERY STICKS, 2 FINELY DICED SHALLOTS, 2 FINELY CHOPPED GARLIC CLOVES, 2 TBSP SUN-DRIED TOMATO PURÉE AND 2 TSP DRIED MIXED HERBS IN A HEAVY-BASED SAUCEPAN WITH 1 LITRE HOT VEGETABLE STOCK AND BRING TO THE BOIL.

COOK, UNCOVERED, OVER A MEDIUM HEAT FOR 10–12 MINUTES. STIR IN 2 X 400 G CANS BLACK-EYED BEANS, RINSED AND DRAINED, AND BRING BACK TO THE BOIL. SEASON, REMOVE FROM THE HEAT AND SERVE WITH CRUSTY BREAD.

HEARTY MINESTRONE
THIS IS NO ORDINARY SOUP –
IT'S A MEAL IN A BOWL!

3 CARROTS, ROUGHLY CHOPPED
1 RED ONION, ROUGHLY CHOPPED
6 CELERY STICKS, ROUGHLY CHOPPED
2 TBSP OLIVE OIL
2 GARLIC CLOVES, FINELY CHOPPED
200 G POTATOES, PEELED AND CUT
   INTO 1-CM DICE
4 TBSP TOMATO PURÉE
1.5 LITRES VEGETABLE STOCK
400 G CAN CHOPPED TOMATOES
150 G SMALL SOUP PASTA
400 G CAN CANNELLINI BEANS,
   RINSED AND DRAINED
100 G BABY SPINACH
SALT AND PEPPER
CRUSTY BREAD, TO SERVE

SERVES 4 WARRIORS
PREP TIME: 15 MINUTES
COOKING TIME: 15-20 MINUTES

WHIZZ THE CARROTS, ONION AND CELERY IN A FOOD PROCESSOR UNTIL FINELY CHOPPED.

AS WITH OTHER RECIPES, IF YOU DON'T HAVE A FOOD PROCESSOR YOU CAN VERY FINELY CHOP ALL THE VEGETABLES WITH A SHARP KNIFE.

EXACTLY - IT'S A CHUNKY SOUP SO THAT'S FINE.

HEAT THE OIL IN A LARGE SAUCEPAN, ADD THE CHOPPED VEGETABLES, GARLIC, POTATOES, TOMATO PUREÉ, STOCK, TOMATOES AND PASTA TO THE PAN.

BRING TO THE BOIL THEN REDUCE THE HEAT, COVER THE PAN AND SIMMER FOR 12-15 MINUTES.

WHEN YOU COOK ALL THE VEGETABLES TOGETHER LIKE THIS IT PRESERVES THE *NUTRIENTS* SO THIS IS A HEALTHY MEAL.

ADD THE CANNELLINI BEANS AND THE SPINACH FOR THE FINAL 2 MINUTES OF COOKING TIME.

LOOKS LIKE I WOKE UP JUST IN TIME.

YOU'RE VERY GOOD AT DOING THAT!

SEASON TO TASTE WITH SALT AND PEPPER.

ADD A LITTLE AT A TIME AND TASTE AS YOU GO UNTIL YOU GET IT JUST HOW YOU WANT IT.

YOU TOOK YOUR TIME, WE'RE READY TO EAT.

SORRY, THERE WAS A QUEUE.

AND YOU HAVE TO HAVE *BREAD* WITH SOUP.

THIS IS A FILLING SOUP SO YOU CAN HAVE IT FOR LUNCH *OR* DINNER.

OR *BOTH* IF YOU MAKE ENOUGH!

VARIATION

BEAN, SPINACH AND PASTA SALAD

RINSE AND DRAIN A 400 G CAN CANNELLINI BEANS AND TIP THE BEANS INTO A LARGE, WIDE BOWL WITH 100 G BABY SPINACH, 2 COARSELY GRATED CARROTS, A THINLY SLICED RED ONION AND 200 G COOKED SHORT PASTA. POUR OVER 2 TBSP RED WINE VINEGAR AND 4 TBSP OLIVE OIL, SEASON WELL, MIX TOGETHER AND SERVE.

CHUNKY PASTA SAUCE
THIS IS A CLASSIC SAUCE THAT YOU CAN ADAPT
TO USE WITH LOTS OF DIFFERENT DISHES.

2 TBSP OLIVE OIL
2 GARLIC CLOVES, CHOPPED
1 RED ONION, CHOPPED
2 CELERY STICKS, CHOPPED
1 CARROT, CHOPPED
400 G CAN CHOPPED TOMATOES
375 G DRIED PENNE
100 G BABY SPINACH
200 G DRAINED CANNED BORLOTTI
    OR KIDNEY BEANS
GRATED PARMESAN CHEESE, TO SERVE

SERVES 4 WARRIORS
PREP TIME: 15 MINUTES
COOKING TIME: 15-20 MINUTES

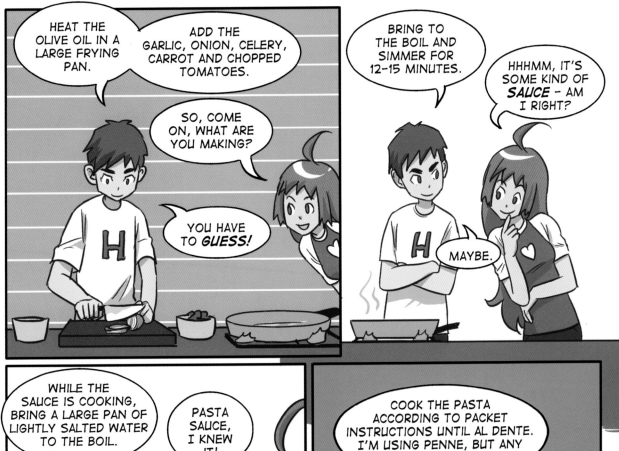

STIR THE SPINACH INTO THE SAUCE AND SEASON WELL.

IT LOOKS LIKE YOU'RE ADDING A HUGE AMOUNT OF SPINACH BUT IT WILTS DOWN VERY QUICKLY.

NOW ADD THE BORLOTTI BEANS AND GIVE THE SAUCE A REALLY GOOD STIR.

CAT'S RIGHT, THE SPINACH REALLY DOES SHRINK DOWN A LOT.

I'M *ALWAYS* RIGHT.

DRAIN THE PASTA AND RETURN IT TO THE PAN.

POUR THE SAUCE OVER THE PASTA AND GENTLY STIR SO THE SAUCE IS MIXED THROUGH EVENLY.

SERVE THE PASTA IMMEDIATELY WITH GRATED PARMESAN SPRINKLED OVER THE TOP.

EXTRA CHEESE FOR ME PLEASE.

WHY NOT MAKE TWICE THE AMOUNT AND FREEZE HALF FOR ANOTHER TIME? THIS WOULD ALSO MAKE AN AWESOME JACKET POTATO FILLING.

QUICK ONE-POT RATATOUILLE
ENJOY THIS MEDLEY OF MEDITERRANEAN VEGETABLES.

100 ML OLIVE OIL
2 ONIONS, CHOPPED
1 AUBERGINE, CUT INTO BITE-SIZED PIECES
2 LARGE COURGETTES, CUT INTO BITE-SIZED PIECES
1 RED PEPPER, CORED, DESEEDED AND CUT INTO
   BITE-SIZED PIECES
1 YELLOW PEPPER, CORED, DESEEDED AND CUT INTO
   BITE-SIZED PIECES
2 GARLIC CLOVES, FINELY CHOPPED
400 G CAN CHOPPED TOMATOES
4 TBSP CHOPPED BASIL
SALT AND PEPPER

TO SERVE:
CRUSTY BREAD
SALAD

SERVES 4 WARRIORS
PREP TIME: 10 MINUTES
COOKING TIME: 25 MINUTES

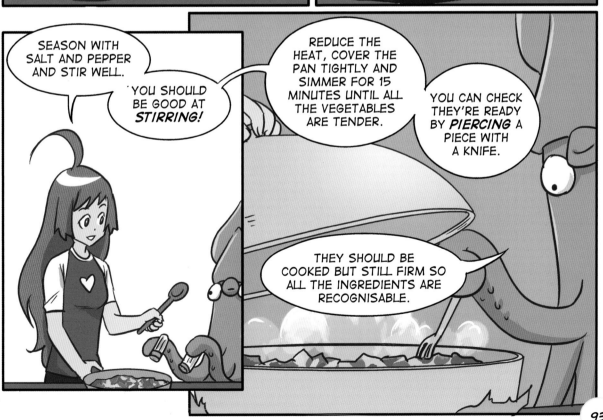

REMOVE THE PAN FROM THE HEAT.

STIR IN THE CHOPPED BASIL.

IT'S REALLY **EASY** TO GROW YOUR OWN BASIL AND YOU'LL SAVE **MONEY**, TOO. YOU CAN GROW IT IN POTS ON A WINDOWSILL IF YOU DON'T HAVE A GARDEN.

IS THAT RATATOUILLE I CAN SMELL?

WE'VE BEEN COOKING ALL AFTERNOON.

YOU CAN'T FOOL ME, I KNOW HOW EASY THIS RECIPE IS!

YOU CAN SERVE THIS WITH BREAD AND A SIDE SALAD.

OR TRY IT WITH SOME GRILLED **HALLOUMI** CHEESE ON TOP, **DELICIOUS!**

EAT IMMEDIATELY IF YOU LIKE OR YOU CAN SERVE IT COLD.

HOT TODAY, COLD TOMORROW.

GREEK-STYLE OMELETTE
THE CLASSIC OMELETTE IS GIVEN A SUMMERY TWIST.

8 LARGE EGGS
1 TSP DRIED OREGANO
1 TBSP FINELY CHOPPED MINT
4 TBSP FINELY CHOPPED PARSLEY
2 TBSP OLIVE OIL
2 SMALL RED ONIONS, ROUGHLY CHOPPED
2 LARGE RIPE TOMATOES, ROUGHLY CHOPPED
½ COURGETTE, ROUGHLY CHOPPED
100 G BLACK OLIVES, PITTED
100 G FETA CHEESE
SALT AND PEPPER
BREAD OR GREEN SALAD, TO SERVE

SERVES 4 WARRIORS
PREP TIME: 15 MINUTES
COOKING TIME: 15-20 MINUTES

REDUCE THE HEAT TO MEDIUM AND POUR THE EGGS INTO THE FRYING PAN.

COOK FOR 3-4 MINUTES, STIRRING AS THE EGGS START TO SET, UNTIL THEY ARE FIRM BUT STILL A LITTLE RUNNY IN PLACES.

WHY DO YOU NEED TO STIR THE EGGS WHILE THEY'RE COOKING?

SO THEY MIX WITH ALL THE OTHER INGREDIENTS. IT ALSO HELPS TO MAKE A FLUFFY OMELETTE.

SCATTER OVER THE FETA, THEN PLACE THE PAN UNDER THE PREHEATED GRILL FOR 4-5 MINUTES OR UNTIL THE OMELETTE IS PUFFED UP AND GOLDEN.

CAN YOU USE ANY CHEESE?

SURE, YOU COULD USE CUBES OF *HALLOUMI* OR *CHEDDAR* IF YOU PREFER.

CUT THE OMELETTE INTO WEDGES.

SERVE WITH A SIMPLE GREEN SALAD IF YOU LIKE.

OR SOME BREAD.

VARIATION

CLASSIC GREEK SALAD

THINLY SLICE 2 RED ONIONS, 4 TOMATOES AND 1 CUCUMBER AND PLACE IN A WIDE SALAD BOWL WITH 200 G CUBED FETA CHEESE AND 100 G PITTED BLACK OLIVES.

DRIZZLE OVER 6 TBSP OLIVE OIL AND SPRINKLE OVER 1 TSP DRIED OREGANO. SEASON, MIX WELL AND SERVE.

SPINACH &
MUSHROOM LASAGNE
A CLASSIC FLAVOUR COMBINATION TO IMPRESS
VEGETARIANS AND MEAT-EATERS ALIKE.

3 TBSP EXTRA VIRGIN OLIVE OIL, PLUS
   EXTRA FOR GREASING
500 G MIXED MUSHROOMS, SLICED
200 G MASCARPONE CHEESE
12 SHEETS OF FRESH LASAGNE
150 G TALEGGIO CHEESE, DERINDED
   AND CUT INTO CUBES
125 G BABY SPINACH LEAVES
SALT AND PEPPER
TOMATO AND ONION SALAD, TO SERVE (OPTIONAL)

SERVES 4 WARRIORS
PREP TIME: 15 MINUTES
COOKING TIME: 10 MINUTES

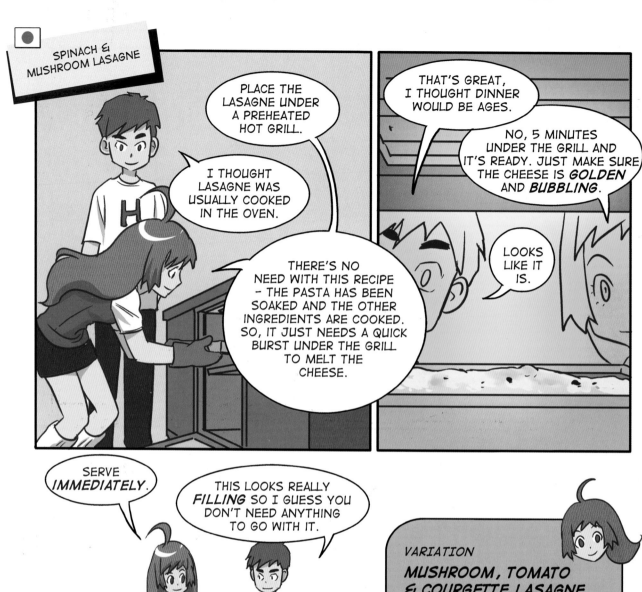

PLACE THE LASAGNE UNDER A PREHEATED HOT GRILL.

I THOUGHT LASAGNE WAS USUALLY COOKED IN THE OVEN.

THERE'S NO NEED WITH THIS RECIPE – THE PASTA HAS BEEN SOAKED AND THE OTHER INGREDIENTS ARE COOKED. SO, IT JUST NEEDS A QUICK BURST UNDER THE GRILL TO MELT THE CHEESE.

THAT'S GREAT, I THOUGHT DINNER WOULD BE AGES.

NO, 5 MINUTES UNDER THE GRILL AND IT'S READY. JUST MAKE SURE THE CHEESE IS *GOLDEN* AND *BUBBLING*.

LOOKS LIKE IT IS.

SERVE *IMMEDIATELY*.

THIS LOOKS REALLY *FILLING* SO I GUESS YOU DON'T NEED ANYTHING TO GO WITH IT.

IT'S FINE ON ITS OWN BUT A TOMATO AND ONION SALAD WOULD BE NICE IF IT'S A SPECIAL MEAL WITH FRIENDS.

THERE'S NO SALAD HERE – ARE YOU SAYING WE AREN'T SPECIAL?!

VARIATION

MUSHROOM, TOMATO & COURGETTE LASAGNE

USE 500 G TOMATOES AND 2 COURGETTES INSTEAD OF THE SPINACH. DROP THE TOMATOES IN A SAUCEPAN OF BOILING WATER FOR 1 MINUTE, THEN SKIN AND SLICE THEM. VERY THINLY SLICE THE COURGETTES BEFORE PROCEEDING WITH THE RECIPE.

QUICK CAULIFLOWER CHEESE
CAULIFLOWER CHEESE IS THE ULTIMATE COMFORT FOOD.

1 CAULIFLOWER, BROKEN INTO LARGE PIECES
50 G PLAIN FLOUR
25 G BUTTER, PLUS EXTRA FOR GREASING
1 TSP MUSTARD POWDER (OPTIONAL)
450 ML MILK
200 G CHEESE, GRATED
  (RED LEICESTER OR CHEDDAR WORK WELL)
SALT AND PEPPER

TO SERVE:
GREEN SALAD
CRUSTY BREAD

SERVES 4 WARRIORS
PREP TIME: 10 MINUTES
COOKING TIME: 15 MINUTES

BRING A LARGE PAN OF LIGHTLY SALTED WATER TO THE BOIL.

COOK THE CAULIFLOWER FOR 7-8 MINUTES UNTIL JUST TENDER. DRAIN WELL.

YOU CAN LEAVE THE COLANDER OF CAULIFLOWER OVER A PAN TO KEEP DRAINING WHILE YOU MAKE THE SAUCE.

THAT'S A GOOD IDEA.

PLACE THE FLOUR, BUTTER AND MUSTARD POWDER, IF USING, IN A MEDIUM-SIZED SAUCEPAN WITH THE MILK.

SLOWLY BRING TO THE BOIL, STIRRING CONSTANTLY, UNTIL SMOOTH AND THICKENED.

TAKE YOUR TIME WITH THIS OR YOU'LL END UP WITH A *LUMPY* SAUCE.

STIR IN HALF THE CHEESE AND, ONCE IT HAS MELTED, SEASON TO TASTE WITH SALT AND PEPPER.

THE CHEESE THICKENS UP THE SAUCE SO DON'T WORRY IF IT IS A LITTLE RUNNY AT FIRST.

TIP THE CAULIFLOWER INTO A BUTTERED OVENPROOF DISH, POUR OVER THE CHEESY SAUCE AND SPRINKLE OVER THE REMAINING CHEESE.

USE A BRUSH TO BUTTER THE DISH OR TEAR OFF A PIECE OF THE BUTTER WRAPPER, SPOON SOME BUTTER ON IT AND USE THE WRAPPER TO SMEAR AROUND THE INSIDE OF THE DISH.

COOK THE CAULIFLOWER CHEESE UNDER A PREHEATED MEDIUM-HOT GRILL FOR 3-4 MINUTES UNTIL *GOLDEN*.

THAT SMELLS GOOD ALREADY.

YOU CAN COOK THIS IN A PREHEATED OVEN IF YOU PREFER.

COOK AT 200°C (400°F), GAS MARK 6, FOR 10-12 MINUTES, UNTIL IT'S BUBBLING AND GOLDEN.

I'LL STICK WITH THE GRILL; IT'LL BE READY SOONER!

IS THIS TO GO WITH THE CAULIFLOWER CHEESE?

YES, THANKS.

I'LL WASH THE LETTUCE AND FIND SOME NICE CRUSTY BREAD.

VARIATION

HEARTY POTATO & CAULIFLOWER SOUP

MELT 25 G BUTTER IN A LARGE PAN WITH 1 TBSP VEGETABLE OIL AND COOK 1 FINELY CHOPPED ONION AND 2 LARGE POTATOES, PEELED AND DICED, OVER A MEDIUM HEAT FOR 8-10 MINUTES UNTIL THE ONION IS SOFTENED AND LIGHTLY GOLDEN.

STIR IN 1 TSP CUMIN SEEDS AND 1 SMALL CAULIFLOWER, BROKEN INTO FLORETS. COOK, STIRRING FREQUENTLY, FOR 3-4 MINUTES, UNTIL THE CAULIFLOWER BEGINS TO SOFTEN SLIGHTLY. POUR IN 900 ML VEGETABLE STOCK AND BRING TO THE BOIL. REDUCE THE HEAT, COVER AND SIMMER GENTLY FOR ABOUT 15 MINUTES UNTIL THE VEGETABLES ARE TENDER. BLEND WITH A HAND-HELD BLENDER UNTIL SMOOTH OR PRESS THROUGH A SIEVE OR COLANDER. SEASON TO TASTE AND LADLE INTO BOWLS.

POTATO GRATIN
WITH JUST A HANDFUL OF INGREDIENTS
YOU CAN CREATE A DELICIOUS DINNER.

625 G POTATOES, THINLY SLICED
500 G SPINACH LEAVES
BUTTER, FOR GREASING
200 G MOZZARELLA CHEESE, GRATED
4 TOMATOES, SLICED
3 EGGS, BEATEN
300 ML WHIPPING CREAM
SALT AND PEPPER

TO SERVE:
SALAD
CRUSTY BREAD

SERVES 4 WARRIORS
PREP TIME: 10 MINUTES
COOKING TIME: 35 MINUTES

IF THERE ARE THICK SKINS ON YOUR POTATOES, YOU MIGHT WANT TO PEEL THEM BEFORE SLICING.

PERSONALLY I PREFER THE SKINS LEFT *ON* – THEY'RE THE BEST BIT!

COOK THE POTATOES IN A LARGE SAUCEPAN OF LIGHTLY SALTED BOILING WATER FOR 5 MINUTES, THEN DRAIN WELL.

WHILE THEY'RE COOKING, YOU CAN COOK THE SPINACH IN A SEPARATE SAUCEPAN OF BOILING WATER FOR 1–2 MINUTES.

DRAIN THE SPINACH AND SQUEEZE OUT THE EXCESS WATER.

GREASE A LARGE OVENPROOF DISH WITH BUTTER.

CHECK OUT THE TIP IN THE CAULIFLOWER CHEESE RECIPE (PAGE 105) TO FIND OUT HOW TO DO THIS.

LINE THE BOTTOM OF THE DISH WITH HALF THE POTATO SLICES.

COVER THE POTATOES WITH THE SPINACH AND HALF THE MOZZARELLA, SEASONING EACH LAYER WELL WITH SALT AND PEPPER.

I FIND IT TRICKY TO GRATE MOZZARELLA, AS IT'S SO SOFT.

IF YOU PREFER YOU CAN VERY FINELY SLICE IT INSTEAD OF GRATING.

COVER WITH THE REMAINING POTATO SLICES AND ARRANGE THE TOMATO SLICES ON TOP.

MMMM, THESE TOMATOES ARE *LOVELY*.

THEY'RE PLUM TOMATOES BUT YOU CAN USE ANY VARIETY YOU LIKE.

SPRINKLE WITH THE REMAINING MOZZARELLA.

I'M GETTING A GOOD FEELING ABOUT THIS DISH.

I'M GETTING A *HUNGRY* FEELING.

IT'S NICE HAVING HELPERS!

WHISK THE EGGS AND CREAM TOGETHER IN A BOWL AND SEASON WELL WITH SALT AND PEPPER.

POUR OVER THE INGREDIENTS IN THE DISH.

BAKE IN A PREHEATED OVEN 180°C (350°F), GAS MARK 4, FOR ABOUT 30 MINUTES.

SERVE WITH A SALAD AND SOME CRUSTY BREAD.

YOU'D SERVE SALAD WITH *DESSERT* IF YOU COULD.

MIXED BEAN KEDGEREE

THIS IS A VEGETARIAN VERSION OF THE ANGLO-INDIAN BREAKFAST DISH SO WHY NOT SWAP YOUR CORNFLAKES FOR KEDGEREE?

INGREDIENTS:
2 TBSP OLIVE OIL
1 ONION, CHOPPED
2 TBSP MILD CURRY POWDER
250 G LONG-GRAIN RICE
750 ML VEGETABLE STOCK
4 EGGS
2 X 400 G CANS MIXED BEANS,
  RINSED AND DRAINED
150 ML SOURED CREAM
SALT AND PEPPER

TO GARNISH:
2 TOMATOES, FINELY CHOPPED
CHOPPED PARSLEY

SERVES 4 WARRIORS
PREP TIME: 10 MINUTES
COOKING TIME: 25 MINUTES

HEAT THE OIL IN A LARGE SAUCEPAN, ADD THE ONION AND COOK GENTLY UNTIL SOFT.

STIR IN THE CURRY POWDER AND RICE.

ARE YOU *REALLY* GOING TO HAVE THIS FOR BREAKFAST?

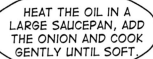

SURE, WHY NOT? BUT IT WOULD BE GREAT FOR DINNER, TOO.

ADD THE STOCK AND SEASON WITH SALT AND PEPPER.

BRING TO THE BOIL, THEN REDUCE THE HEAT, COVER AND SIMMER, STIRRING OCCASIONALLY, FOR 10-15 MINUTES UNTIL ALL THE STOCK HAS BEEN ABSORBED AND THE RICE IS *TENDER*.

IF THE RICE IS DRYING OUT, YOU CAN ADD A LITTLE MORE STOCK OR BOILED WATER TO THE DISH. ADD A LITTLE AT A TIME, AS YOU DON'T WANT IT TO BE TOO WET.

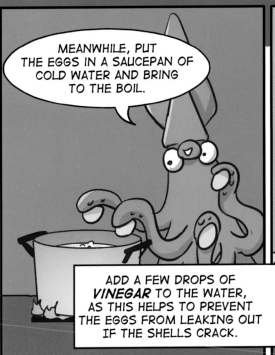

MEANWHILE, PUT THE EGGS IN A SAUCEPAN OF COLD WATER AND BRING TO THE BOIL.

ADD A FEW DROPS OF *VINEGAR* TO THE WATER, AS THIS HELPS TO PREVENT THE EGGS FROM LEAKING OUT IF THE SHELLS CRACK.

COOK THE EGGS FOR 10 MINUTES, THEN RINSE IN COLD WATER, REFILL THE PAN WITH COLD WATER AND LEAVE TO COOL.

WHY DO YOU NEED TO DO THAT?

IT STOPS THE COOKING PROCESS SO THE EGGS STAY NICE AND *SOFT* IN THE MIDDLE.

ONION & MUSHROOM QUESADILLAS
THESE MAKE A GREAT POST-PARTY SNACK
OR AN EASY MEAL FOR MATES.

INGREDIENTS:
3 TBSP OLIVE OIL
2 RED ONIONS, THINLY SLICED
1 TSP CASTER SUGAR
200 G BUTTON MUSHROOMS, SLICED
8 SMALL SOFT FLOUR TORTILLAS
150 G CHEDDAR CHEESE, GRATED
SMALL HANDFUL OF PARSLEY, CHOPPED
SALT AND PEPPER
GREEN SALAD, TO SERVE (OPTIONAL)

SERVES 4 WARRIORS
PREP TIME: 10 MINUTES
COOKING TIME: ABOUT 30 MINUTES

SWEET STUFF

PINEAPPLE WITH LIME & CHILLI SYRUP
A QUICK AND ELEGANT DESSERT BURSTING WITH FLAVOURS.

1 BABY PINEAPPLE
100 G CASTER SUGAR
100 ML WATER
3 SMALL RED CHILLIES, DESEEDED
   AND CHOPPED
GRATED RIND AND JUICE OF 1 LIME
ICE CREAM, TO SERVE

SERVES 4 WARRIORS
PREP TIME: 10 MINUTES, PLUS COOLING
COOKING TIME: 10 MINUTES

123

PINEAPPLE WITH LIME & CHILLI SYRUP

ONCE IT'S COOLED DOWN YOU CAN STIR IN THE LIME RIND AND JUICE.

LAY THE PINEAPPLE SLICES ON A PLATE AND DRIZZLE THE SYRUP OVER.

IT MIGHT BE EASIER TO PUT IT IN A JUG FIRST.

I THINK I CAN *MANAGE*.

I LOVE THIS WITH A SCOOP OF ICE CREAM.

YES, IT WORKS WELL WITH THE *HEAT* FROM THE CHILLI.

VARIATION

PEARS WITH CINNAMON SYRUP

PEEL 4 RIPE PEARS, CUT INTO QUARTERS AND REMOVE THE CORES. PUT IN A SAUCEPAN, POUR OVER WATER TO COVER AND ADD THE CASTER SUGAR AS ABOVE, WITH THE GRATED RIND AND JUICE OF 1 LEMON, 1 CINNAMON STICK AND 6 CLOVES.

SIMMER, TURNING OCCASIONALLY, FOR 10 MINUTES OR UNTIL THE PEAR PIECES ARE TENDER. REMOVE THE PEARS WITH A SLOTTED SPOON AND SET ASIDE. BRING THE LIQUID TO THE BOIL AND BOIL RAPIDLY UNTIL IT IS SYRUPY. LEAVE TO COOL, THEN POUR OVER THE PEARS.

BANOFFEE CHOCOLATE MUFFINS
CHOCOLATE AND BANANA IS A WINNING COMBINATION.

225 G SELF-RAISING FLOUR, SIFTED
2 TBSP COCOA POWDER, SIFTED
100 G CASTER SUGAR
100 G DARK CHOCOLATE CHIPS
2 EGGS
2 SMALL RIPE BANANAS
50 ML VEGETABLE OIL
125 G NATURAL YOGURT
READY-MADE TOFFEE SAUCE, TO SERVE

MAKES 12 MUFFINS
PREP TIME: 15 MINUTES
COOKING TIME: 18-22 MINUTES

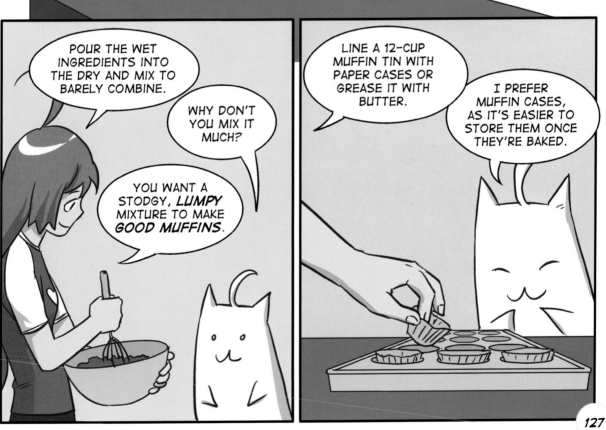

RASPBERRY MUFFINS
THESE ARE IDEAL FOR TAKING INTO COLLEGE FOR A MID-MORNING SNACK.

200 G PLAIN FLOUR, SIFTED
75 G CASTER SUGAR
2 TBSP GROUND ALMONDS
2 TSP BAKING POWDER
GRATED RIND OF 1 LEMON
50 G BUTTER, MELTED
150 ML BUTTERMILK
1 EGG, BEATEN
150 G FRESH OR FROZEN RASPBERRIES

MAKES 6 MUFFINS
PREP TIME: 15 MINUTES
COOKING TIME: 15-20 MINUTES

MIX TOGETHER THE FLOUR, SUGAR, GROUND ALMONDS, BAKING POWDER AND LEMON RIND IN A LARGE BOWL.

WHEN YOU GRATE THE LEMON, MAKE SURE YOU ONLY REMOVE THE YELLOW *RIND* AND NOT THE WHITE *PITH* UNDERNEATH IT.

WHAT ARE YOU COOKING IN THE MICROWAVE?

I'M MELTING THE BUTTER BUT IT JUST NEEDS A FEW SECONDS SO I'M KEEPING WATCH.

MIX TOGETHER THE BUTTERMILK, EGG, MELTED BUTTER AND RASPBERRIES IN A JUG.

DO YOU NEED TO DEFROST FROZEN RASPBERRIES?

NO, YOU WANT TO HAVE PIECES OF RASPBERRY IN THE MUFFINS SO YOU DON'T WANT THEM TO COLLAPSE COMPLETELY. YOU MIGHT NEED TO COOK THEM A LITTLE LONGER THOUGH.

ADD THE RASPBERRY MIXTURE TO THE DRY INGREDIENTS IN THE BOWL.

STIR EVERYTHING TOGETHER USING A LARGE METAL SPOON.

DON'T MIX UNTIL IT'S COMPLETELY SMOOTH – YOU WANT IT JUST COMBINED AND SLIGHTLY LUMPY.

CHOCOLATE CHIP COOKIES
THIS IS THE ONLY COOKIE RECIPE
YOU'LL EVER NEED!

125 G SOFT UNSALTED BUTTER, DICED
175 G SOFT LIGHT BROWN SUGAR
1 TSP VANILLA EXTRACT
1 EGG, LIGHTLY BEATEN
1 TBSP MILK
200 G PLAIN FLOUR
1 TSP BAKING POWDER
250 G DARK CHOCOLATE CHIPS

MAKES 16 COOKIES
PREP TIME: 10 MINUTES, PLUS COOLING
COOKING TIME: 15 MINUTES

LINE A LARGE BAKING SHEET WITH NONSTICK BAKING PAPER.

THE EASIEST WAY TO DO THIS IS TO DRAW AROUND THE BASE OF THE TIN ONTO THE PAPER THEN CUT OUT INSIDE THE PENCIL LINE.

IN A LARGE BOWL, BEAT THE BUTTER AND SUGAR TOGETHER UNTIL LIGHT AND FLUFFY.

YOU CAN USE A FORK TO DO THIS BUT A WHISK IS BETTER, IF YOU HAVE ONE, AS YOU'LL GET A FLUFFIER MIXTURE.

STIR IN THE VANILLA EXTRACT, THEN GRADUALLY ADD THE EGG, BEATING WELL AFTER EACH ADDITION.

STIR IN THE MILK.

VANILLA EXTRACT IS MORE *EXPENSIVE* THAN VANILLA ESSENCE, AS IT ACTUALLY COMES FROM A VANILLA POD. HOWEVER, YOU ONLY USE A SMALL AMOUNT SO IT LASTS A LONG TIME.

SIFT THE FLOUR AND BAKING POWDER INTO A SEPARATE BOWL, THEN FOLD INTO THE BUTTER AND EGG MIXTURE.

STIR IN THE CHOCOLATE CHIPS.

CAN I DO THAT?

SURE!

VICTORIA SPONGE MUG CAKE

A CAKE COOKED IN A MUG
– WHAT COULD BE SIMPLER?

3 TBSP VERY SOFT BUTTER
2 TBSP CASTER SUGAR, PLUS EXTRA
   FOR SPRINKLING
1 EGG YOLK, OR ½ BEATEN EGG
4 TBSP SELF-RAISING FLOUR
¼ TSP VANILLA EXTRACT
1 TBSP STRAWBERRY JAM

SERVES 1 WARRIOR
PREP TIME: 3 MINUTES
COOKING TIME: 1½ MINUTES

ACKNOWLEDGEMENTS

For Eva and Quinn - my two kitchen ninjas in training.